5-Finger Fun!

Starter Solos for Keyboard
Lynn Freeman Olson

Contents

Alfred

I Love a Parade

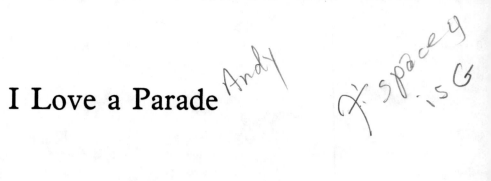

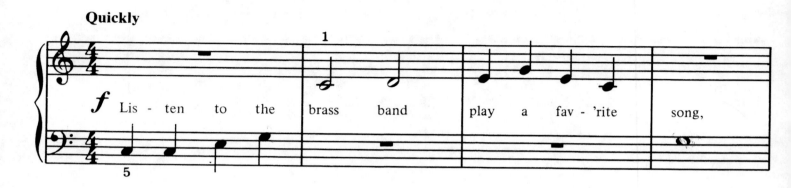

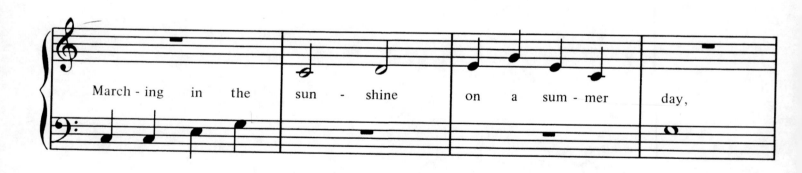

TROMBONE SECTION

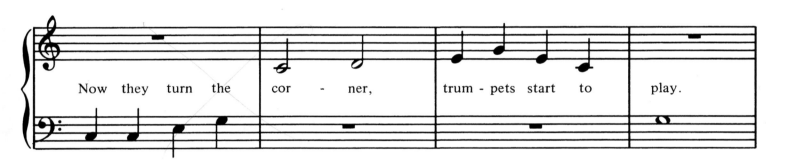

Now they turn the cor - ner, trum - pets start to play.

On - ly a pa - rade can make me feel this way!

BIG FINISH!

4

My Friend Sammy

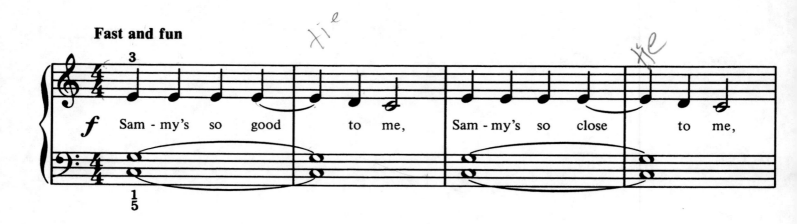

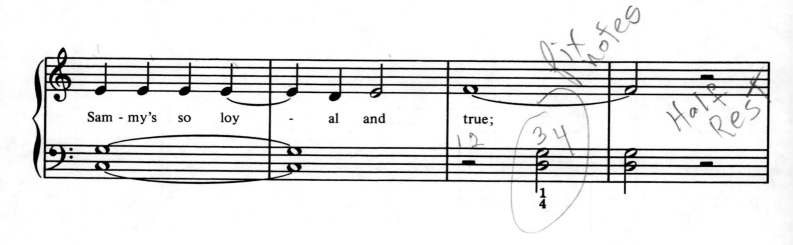

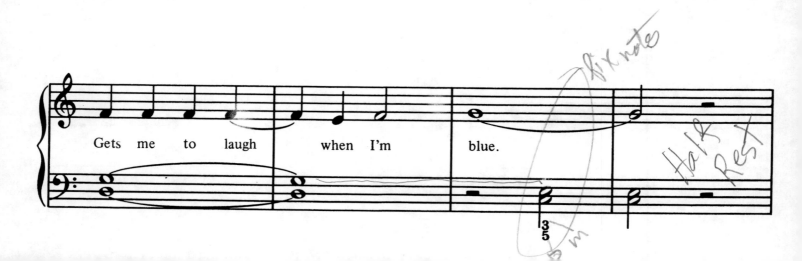

If I for - get to be glad for a - while,

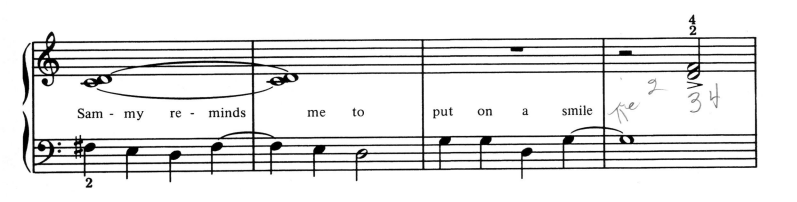

Sam - my re - minds me to put on a smile

Sam - my's a friend who's right, all through the day and night.

Sure, he's a dog! and he's mine!

When the Saints Go Marching In

Traditional
Arr. L.F.O.

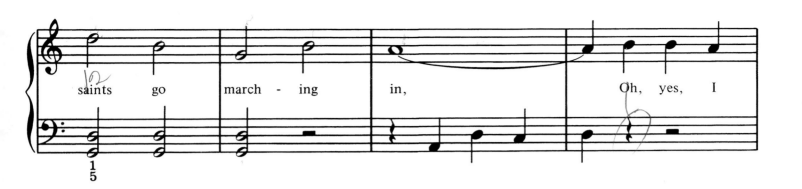

saints go march - ing in, Oh, yes, I

want to be in their num - ber, When the

saints go march - ing in!

OCTAVE HIGHER

OCTAVE LOWER

Oats, Peas, Beans . . . and Blues!

Traditional
Arr. L.F.O.

Rocking along

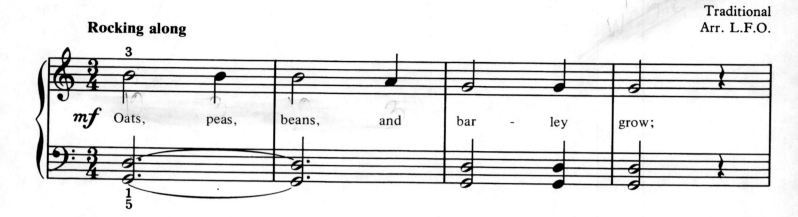

mf Oats,   peas,   beans,   and   bar - ley   grow;

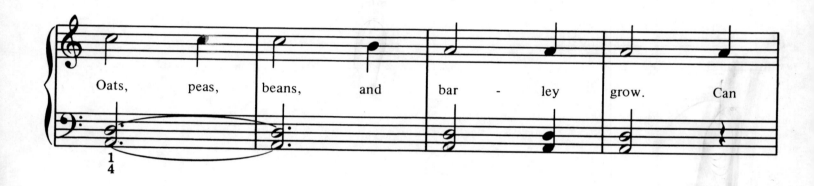

Oats,   peas,   beans,   and   bar - ley   grow.   Can

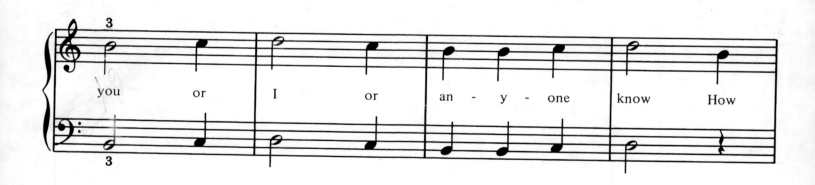

you   or   I   or   an - y - one   know   How

oats,   peas   beans,   and   bar - ley   grow?

Echo in Blue

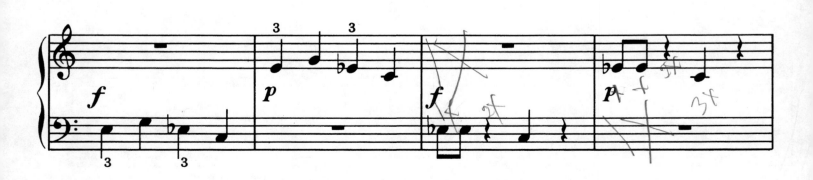

ALMOST AN ECHO

Lightly Row

Traditional Folksong

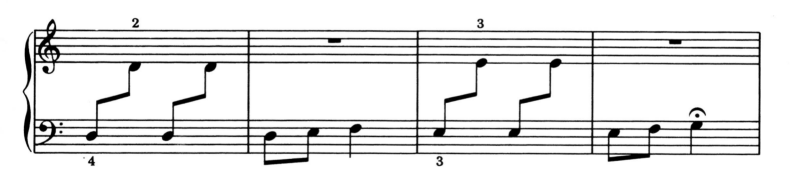

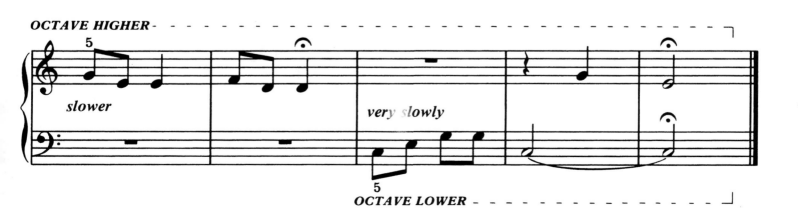

14

Sidewalks of New York

Lawler and Blake
Arr. L.F.O.

"Lon - don Bridge is fall - ing down."

Boys and girls to - geth - er, Me and

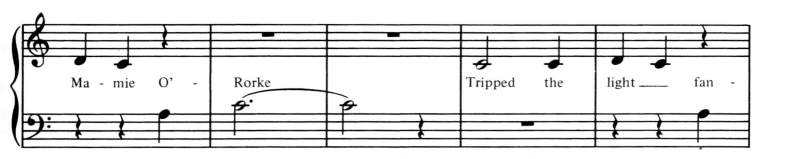

Ma - mie O' - Rorke Tripped the light ___ fan -

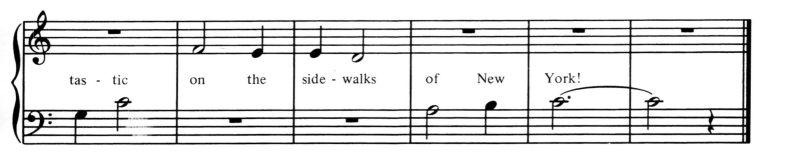

tas - tic on the side - walks of New York!

Music for the Clowns

Fast and funny

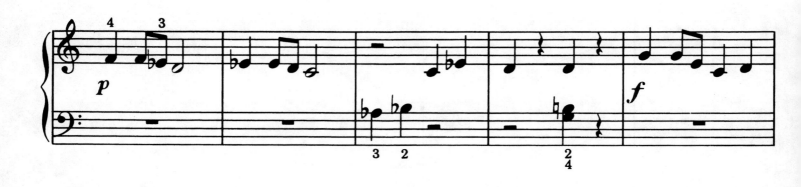

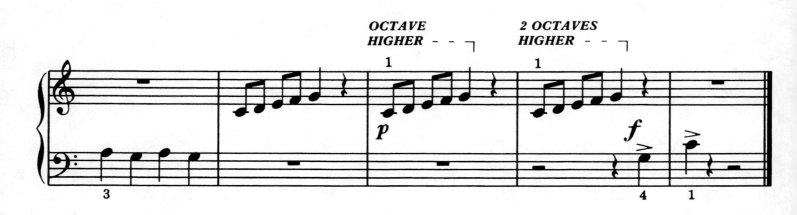